# Changing Materials
# Heating

**Chris Oxlade**

**www.heinemannlibrary.co.uk**
Visit our website to find out more information about Heinemann Library books.

**To order:**
☎ Phone +44 (0) 1865 888066
📄 Fax +44 (0) 1865 314091
💻 Visit www.heinemannlibrary.co.uk

Edited by Charlotte Guillan and Catherine Veitch
Designed by Ryan Frieson and Betsy Wernert
Original illustrations © Capstone Global Library Ltd.
Illustrated by Randy Schirz (p. 8)
Illustrated by Hart McLeod (pp. 11)
Photo research by Elizabeth Alexander and Virginia Stroud-Lewis
Originated by Modern Age Repro House Ltd
Printed in China by South China Printing Company Ltd

ISBN 978 0 431 17477 8 (hardback)
13 12 11 10 09
10 9 8 7 6 5 4 3 2 1

**British Library Cataloguing in Publication Data**
Oxlade, Chris
Heating. - (Changing materials)
536
A full catalogue record for this book is available from the British Library.

**Acknowledgements**

We would like to thank the following for permission to reproduce photographs: Alamy **pp. 6** (© Ilya Shadrin), **15** (© Timothy Herzel), **17** (© Adrian Sherratt/Alamy), **21** (Peter Bowater), **23** (© Richard Church), **24** (© superclic), **26** (© foodfolio); © Capstone Global Library **pp. 4, 5** (MM Studios); © Capstone Publishers **pp. 7, 28, 29** (Karon Dubke); Corbis **pp. 13** (© Jason Hosking/zefa), **27** (© Charles O'Rear); iStockphoto **p. 22** (© Leah-Anne Thompson); Photolibrary **p. 10** (Frank Wieder Photography/Fresh Food Images); Science Photo Library **pp. 9** (Martyn F. Chillmaid), **18** (Martin Dohrn); Shutterstock **pp. 12** (© ulga), **14** (© AXL), **16** (© Luis Francisco Cordero), **19** (© CAN BALCIOGLU), **20** (© Stephen Orsillo), **25** (© Trutta55).

Cover photograph of a steaming kettle reproduced with permission of iStockphoto/© Rick Lord.

Every effort has been made to contact copyright holders of material reproduced in this book. Any omissions will be rectified in subsequent printings if notice is given to the publishers.

# Contents

About materials.....................................4

Changing materials...............................6

Different materials................................8

Hot and cold ....................................10

Heating up.......................................12

Melting ...........................................14

Melting points...................................16

Boiling ............................................18

Boiling points ...................................20

Investigating heating up .....................22

Sources of heat ................................24

Changing properties ..........................26

Investigating escaping gas..................28

Glossary ..........................................30

Find out more ...................................31

Index ..............................................32

Words appearing in the text in bold, **like this**, are explained in the glossary.

# About materials

How many different types of materials do you know? Can you see any wood, plastic, or metal in this photo? These are all materials we use to make things.

Can you name the different materials in this photograph?

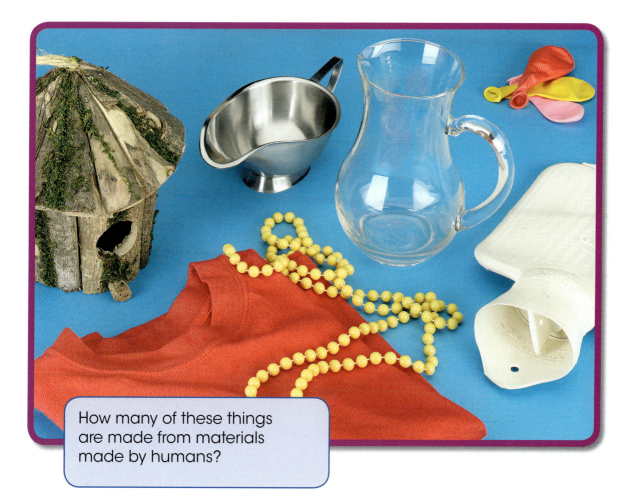

How many of these things are made from materials made by humans?

Some materials are **natural** materials.
We get them from the world around us.
Soil, cotton, and rubber are natural materials.
Humans make other materials, such as glass and metals.

# Changing materials

When water cools down it turns into ice.

Materials can change shape. Sometimes we can change the **properties** of a material. The properties of a material include how it looks and feels.

Materials often change when we heat them up. Heating a material makes it warmer, or hotter.

This ice is **melting** because the child's hands are warming it.

# Different materials

Most materials we see are **solid** materials. But some are **liquids**, like water. And some are **gases**, like the air around us.

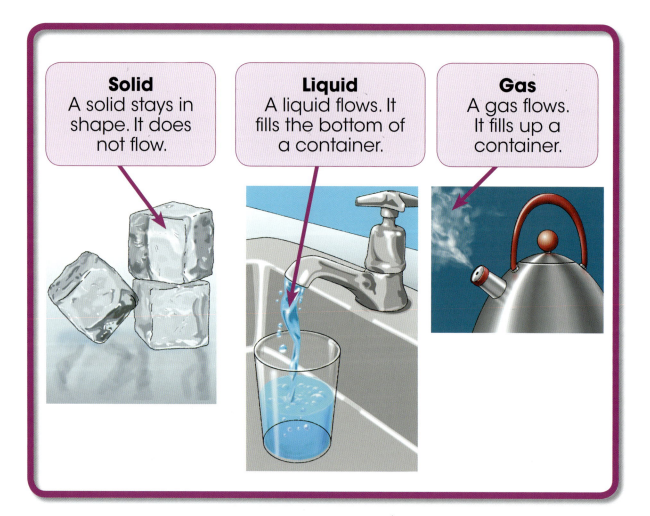

**Solid**
A solid stays in shape. It does not flow.

**Liquid**
A liquid flows. It fills the bottom of a container.

**Gas**
A gas flows. It fills up a container.

When a solid material heats up it can turn into a liquid. When a liquid heats up it can turn into a gas.

When liquid water is heated it turns into bubbles of gas.

# Hot and cold

Some things in the world around us are hot and some are cold. We can tell if things are warm or cool by touching them. But hot things, such as ovens and irons, can burn you, so it is important to be careful.

This food is hot.
The drink is cold.

**Temperature** tells us how cold or how hot something is. The temperature of a cold thing is lower than the temperature of a hot thing. Temperature is measured in degrees Celsius (°C) or degrees Fahrenheit (°F).

We measure temperature with a **thermometer**.

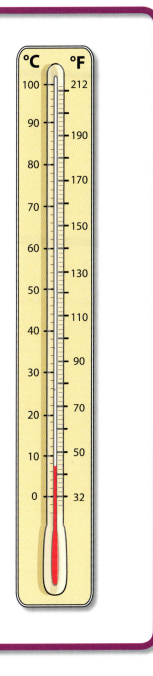

# Heating up

Heat is going into this pan, making it hotter.

To heat up a material we must add heat to it. The heat goes into the material and makes its **temperature** go up.

There are many ways of heating things up. Holding something near a fire makes it warmer. Putting something in an oven or in sunlight also heats it up.

The meat on a barbecue cooks because it is heated by the fire below it.

# Melting

When we warm up some **solid** materials they turn into **liquids**. Ice is a solid. When it warms up, it turns into water, which is a liquid.

Warm weather heats ice and it turns into water.

Solid wax melts
when it is heated
by a candle's flame.

When a solid turns into a liquid it changes.
This change is called **melting**.

# Melting points

The ice is turning into water at 0°C (32°F).

A material always **melts** at the same **temperature**. For example, ice always melts at 0°C (32°F). This is called the **melting point** of ice.

Some materials do not melt until they are at a much higher temperature than 0°C (32°F). For example, pans are made of metal because metal has a very high melting point. The pans will not melt on the stove or in the oven.

This metal is so hot that it is glowing red. It has started to melt and is soft enough to bend.

# Boiling

When we warm up some **liquids** they change into **gases**. For example, water changes into a gas when you heat it up in a pan or kettle. The gas is called steam or **water vapour**.

You can see bubbles of gas in the water as it boils.

The gas that comes from a kettle's spout is steam, or water vapour.

When a liquid turns into a gas, the material changes. This change is called **boiling**.

# Boiling points

A **liquid** always **boils** at the same **temperature**. For example, water always boils at 100°C (212°F). This is called the **boiling point** of water.

Water always turns into steam or **water vapour** at 100°C (212°F).

Other liquids have to be much hotter before they boil. A metal must be very hot before it will boil.

This metal is very hot. It has turned into liquid metal but it is still not hot enough to boil.

# Investigating heating up

When you have been outside on a cold winter day, your hands may feel freezing. How many ways can you think of to warm them up again?

Breathing on your hands warms them up because your breath is warm.

Rubbing your hands together is a way of warming them up. This works because of **friction** between your hands. Rubbing any materials together makes friction and warms them up.

Friction makes heat when you rub your hands.

# Sources of heat

To make something hotter we have to add heat to it. Cooking on an electric hob heats something up.

Heat from the cooker ring makes the water **boil**.

Heat in the Sun's rays makes the sand warm.

The Sun also heats things up. During the day, heat from the Sun warms materials. For example, on a hot day at the beach, the sand feels hot under your feet because the Sun has heated it.

# Changing properties

Heating up a material can change the material's **properties**. Often they cannot be changed back. For example, cake mixture changes when you put it into a hot oven.

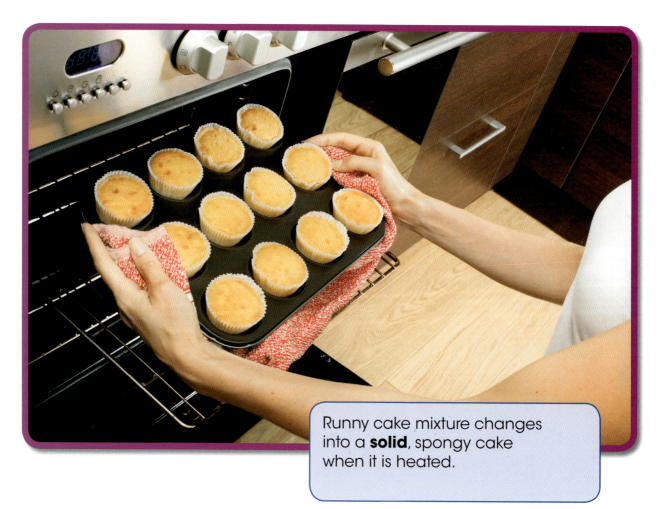

Runny cake mixture changes into a **solid**, spongy cake when it is heated.

When a material is burned we can never get it back. When you put wood on a bonfire, the wood burns and turns to ash. The wood is gone forever.

Wood is changing into ash on top of this fire.

# Investigating escaping gas

This simple experiment will show you that **gases** grow to fill up more space when they are heated.

## You will need:

* a large, empty, plastic drink bottle

* a small coin that will cover the bottle's neck.

## Activity

1) Dip a small coin in water and put it over the bottle's neck.
2) Very gently put your hands around the bottle. Just touch the bottle, without squeezing it.

## What happens

Heat from your hands warms the air in the bottle. The air spreads out and pushes up against the coin, making it jump.

2

# Glossary

**boiling**  when a material changes from liquid to gas

**boiling point**  temperature at which a material always boils

**friction**  force that tries to stop two surfaces sliding against each other

**gas**  material that flows and fills a space. Air is a gas.

**liquid**  material that flows and fills the bottom of a container. Water is a liquid.

**melting**  when a material changes from solid to liquid

**melting point**  temperature at which a material always melts

**natural**  something that is not made by people. It comes from animals, plants, or the rocks of the Earth.

**properties**  things that tell us what a material is like, such as how it feels and looks

**solid**  material that stays in shape and does not flow. Wood is a solid.

**temperature**  measure of how hot or cold something is

**thermometer**  tool for measuring how hot or cold something is

**water vapour**  gas form of water, made when water boils

# Find out more

## Books

*A Sense of Science: Exploring Materials,* Claire Llewellyn (Franklin Watts, 2007)

*Materials series (Cotton, Glass, Metal, Paper, Plastic, Rock, Rubber, Soil, Water, Wood, Wool)* Chris Oxlade (Heinemann Library, 2002)

*Science Alive: Hot and Cold,* Terry Jennings (Franklin Watts, 2008)

*Temperature: Heating Up and Cooling Down,* Darlene R Stille (Picture Window Books, 2004)

## Websites

www.bbc.co.uk/schools/scienceclips

www.bbc.co.uk/schools/podsmission
There are fun materials activities on these BBC websites.

www.crickweb.co.uk/ks1science.html
Visit this website for interactive science activities.

# Index

boiling 18–21, 24
boiling points 20
breath 22

cookers and ovens 10, 13, 17,
    24, 26
cooling 6, 10

fires 13, 27
food 10, 13
friction 23

gases 8, 9, 18, 19
    escaping gas 28–29

hands 7, 22–23
heating up 7, 9, 12–13, 22–23
    boiling 18–21, 24
    heat sources 24–25
    melting 14–15, 16–17
hot and cold 10–11

ice 6, 7, 14, 16

liquids 8, 9, 14, 15, 18, 19, 20, 21

materials
    changing 6–7, 18, 19, 27
    man-made materials 5
    natural materials 5

melting points 16–17
metals 5, 17, 21

pans 12, 17
properties 6
    changing 26–27

sand 25
solids 8, 9, 14, 15, 26
steam 18, 19, 20
Sun 13, 25

temperature 11, 12, 16, 17, 20
    measuring 11
    thermometer 11

water 6, 8, 9, 14, 18, 20, 24
water vapour 18, 19, 20
wax 15
wood 27